Chomp-O-Rama

The Strange Ways That Animals Eat

For my brother, Robert. Here you go!
—M.B.

To Jen, I couldn't do this without you
—K.R.

ACKNOWLEDGEMENTS Huge thanks to the Owlkids team, especially my editor, Stacey Roderick, for your expert editing and positivity as we worked our way through this book. Much gratitude to Kyle Reed for your amazing art. (Somehow it's even cuter than our last book!) Many thanks to Danielle Arbour for such skillful design work. And, as always, thank you to Sam and Grace, my most favorite dinner companions.

Text © 2025 Maria Birmingham | Illustrations © 2025 Kyle Reed

All rights reserved. No part of this publication may be reproduced, stored in a retrieval system, or transmitted in any form or by any means, without the prior written permission of Owlkids Books Inc., or in the case of photocopying or other reprographic copying, a license from the Canadian Copyright Licensing Agency (Access Copyright). For an Access Copyright license, visit www.accesscopyright.ca or call toll-free to 1-800-893-5777.

Owlkids Books acknowledges the financial support of the Canada Council for the Arts, the Ontario Arts Council, the Government of Canada through the Canada Book Fund (CBF) and the Government of Ontario through the Ontario Creates Book Initiative for our publishing activities.

Owlkids Books gratefully acknowledges that our office in Toronto is located on the traditional territory of many nations, including the Mississaugas of the Credit, the Chippewa, the Wendat, the Anishinaabeg, and the Haudenosaunee Peoples.

Published in Canada by Owlkids Books Inc., 1 Eglinton Avenue East, Toronto, ON M4P 3A1
Published in the US by Owlkids Books Inc., 819 Bancroft Way, Berkeley, CA 94710

Library of Congress Control Number: 2024936971

Library and Archives Canada Cataloguing in Publication
Title: Chomp-o-rama : the strange ways that animals eat / written by Maria Birmingham ; illustrated by Kyle Reed.
Names: Birmingham, Maria, author. | Reed, Kyle, illustrator.
Description: Includes bibliographical references.
Identifiers: Canadiana (print) 20240371968 | Canadiana (ebook) 20240371976 |
ISBN 9781771475501 (hardcover) | ISBN 9781771477222 (EPUB)
Subjects: LCSH: Animals—Food—Juvenile literature. | LCSH: Animal behavior—Juvenile literature.
LCGFT: Instructional and educational works. | LCGFT: Illustrated works.
Classification: LCC QL756.5 .B57 2025 | DDC j591.5/3—dc23

Edited by Stacey Roderick | Designed by Danielle Arbour

Manufactured in Guangdong, Dongguan, China, in August 2024, by Toppan Leefung Packaging & Printing (Dongguan) Co., Ltd.   Job #BAYDC139

hc   A   B   C   D   E   F

 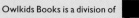 

Chomp-O-Rama

The Strange Ways That Animals Eat

Written by
MARIA BIRMINGHAM

Illustrated by
KYLE REED

Owlkids Books

Crunch ... munch ... slurp ... CHOMP!

It's mealtime for the animals in this book. Each creature has its own way of eating. Some dine in ways similar to you. And others definitely do *not*. Before you go track down a snack for yourself, join these hungry beasts and see the wild ways they gobble up grub.

While you slurp up some soup ...

... a butterfly gulps turtle tears.

Butterflies use the straw-like part on the front of their head to slurp up sweet liquids, such as nectar and sap. But some butterflies in the Amazon rainforest also drink turtle tears! They need the salt found in the tears of yellow-spotted river turtles to stay healthy. Don't worry about the turtles, though. They're not sad. They cry to clean out their eyes!

While you bring a lunch bag to school ...

... a chipmunk carries food in its cheeks.

Busy chipmunks have cheek pouches that are like handy pockets for holding their food, such as nuts and seeds. Each pouch can stretch as big as the chipmunk's head! With its cheeks stuffed full, this critter scurries back to its home and stores away the food it gathered. It'll eat this stash of goodies later, during the cold winter months.

While you put your leftovers in the fridge ...

... a Canada jay stores its scraps in trees.

Canada jays fly from tree to tree searching for meals of fruit, berries, and bugs. They save any extras by sticking them onto a tree. First, the birds take a morsel of food in their mouth to cover it in gooey spit. Then they stick this blob under bark high in the treetops. The jays may do this a thousand times a day! Amazingly, they usually remember their hiding spots.

While you chomp on crunchy snacks ...

... a crocodile gobbles up rocks.

Crocs eat rocks! But it's not because they find them tasty. Crocodiles can't chew like we do, so they swallow their prey whole or in big chunks. That's also why they gulp down small rocks—to grind up that food in their belly! The rocks usually stay in a crocodile's stomach, ready for the next meal. But sometimes the croc will throw them up and swallow a new batch of stones.

While you happily share with your friends ...

... a vampire bat has an unusual way of sharing its food.

Every night, vampire bats fly off to find their meal of choice: the blood of birds and cattle. But sometimes a bat has no luck tracking down food. That's when other bats in its colony help out. Female vampire bats who managed to eat well that night will throw up some of the blood they ate so their hungry friend can slurp it up!

While you eat one meal at a time ...

... a pygmy shrew nibbles all day and all night long.

This little mammal has to eat pretty much nonstop to survive. If it goes even a few hours without food, the pygmy shrew is a goner. So it spends most of its time digging in soft soil looking for prey, such as bugs and spiders. Even at night, the shrew scarfs down a meal about every fifteen minutes, sleeping for just a few moments here and there.

While you shop for food with your family ...

... an Arctic fox steals its meals.

After a long winter without much to eat, the Arctic fox is hungry! Lucky for the fox, spring is when millions of snow geese return to nest. The fox prowls the tundra looking for nests the geese aren't watching over. When it finds one, the sly thief grabs an egg in its mouth and scurries off. It'll snatch many eggs over the spring, burying most to eat in the months ahead.

While you sometimes use a knife to cut up your dinner ...

... a sea otter uses a stone to crack open its meal.

To eat a meal of shelled prey such as clams, crabs, or sea urchins, a sea otter flips onto its back and places a rock on its chest. Then it gets to smashing! It whacks the hard prey on the rock to crack the shell. Now it can gobble up the soft meat inside.

While you take bites of your food ...

... a snake swallows its meal whole.

A rattlesnake eats about every two weeks. But when it's hungry, there's no stopping it. Once it tracks down a meal, such as a mouse or lizard, it strikes fast and plunges its fangs into the animal. The fangs inject venom that stuns the victim. Then the rattler s-t-r-e-t-c-h-e-s open its mouth extra-wide and swallows its meal in one big gulp!

While you grab a snack on the bus ride home ...

... a dragonfly catches bugs as it flies.

For dragonflies, bugs—especially mosquitoes—are a favorite food. A dragonfly will catch them as it swoops through the air. And this skilled hunter rarely misses! Once the bug is in its grasp, it munches down its meal. However, if its prey is on the larger side, a dragonfly may come in for a landing to finish up.

While you munch on all kinds of different foods ...

... a giant panda eats mainly bamboo.

Found only in the forested mountains of China, the giant panda is one picky eater. It gobbles up the leaves, shoots, and stems of bamboo plants and rarely eats anything else. To get enough nutrients, the panda spends at least ten hours a day crunching away.

And while you eat meals with your family ...

... flamingos gather in large flocks to feed.

When they eat, flamingos flock together to wade in lakes and lagoons. Sometimes there are thousands of birds! A flamingo eats by dunking its head under water. It sucks water and mud into its bill. Then it swishes its head from side to side, straining the tiny shrimp or algae from the muddy water before gobbling them up.

That's one hungry group of animals!

While all of these creatures have different eating habits, they do have one thing in common: food is essential to their survival. *You* also need food and its nutrients to survive. It's what keeps you healthy and strong. And it gives your body the energy to think, move, and grow.

Each of the animals in this book has certain foods it must eat to survive. Take the butterfly. Although it may slurp down some turtle tears here and there, its main food is the nectar that comes from plants. Plant-eating creatures such as butterflies are given a special name: *herbivores*. For others, such as the rattlesnake and crocodile, dinner is about meat, meat, and more meat. Animals that eat only meat are called *carnivores*. Finally, there are creatures including the Arctic fox and pygmy shrew who enjoy a variety of foods. They happily gobble up both meat and plants. They are called *omnivores*.

Now that we've got that all straightened out, perhaps it's time to leave these animals to their munching, crunching, and lunching. Besides … do you hear that? All this talk of food is making someone's tummy grumble. And you know what that means …

It's time to CHOMP!

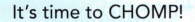

SUGGESTED READING

BEER, JULIE. *Why? Animals: 99+ Awesome Answers for Curious Kids.* New York: National Geographic Kids, 2022.

BIRMINGHAM, MARIA. *Snooze-O-Rama: The Strange Ways That Animals Sleep.* Toronto: Owlkids Books, 2021.

BUNTING, PHILIP. *The World's Most Ridiculous Animals (Volume 2).* London: Happy Yak, 2022.

HEAVENRICH, SUE. *13 Ways to Eat a Fly.* Watertown: Charlesbridge, 2021.

HOARE, BEN. *The Wonders of Nature.* London: Dorling Kindersley Limited, 2019.

LILLEY, MATT. *Good Eating: The Short Life of Krill.* New York: Tilbury House Publishers, 2022.

NATIONAL GEOGRAPHIC KIDS. Online.

SAN DIEGO ZOO. Online.

STAMPS, CAROLINE. *Animal Teams: How Amazing Animals Work Together in the Wild.* London: Dorling Kindersley Limited, 2022.

STEWART, MELISSA. *Whale Fall: Exploring an Ocean-Floor Ecosystem.* New York: Random House Studio, 2023.

SWITCH ZOO. Online.

WILD KRATTS: Creaturepedia. Online.